Day Trading For Beginners Learn The Best Strategies On How To Profit Using Trading Tactics, Tools, Psychology, Money Management And Generate Passive Income

D1799627

Also by Michael Branson

Swing Trading A Beginners And Advanced Guide For Effective Trading Tactics, Make More Money And Reach Financial Freedom Day Trading For Beginners Learn The Best Strategies On How To Profit Using Trading Tactics, Tools, Psychology, Money Management And Generate Passive Income

Table of Contents

Introduction

Maybe you have thought that day trading is a financial activity that is only meant for the chosen few. Well, if this is what you have been thinking, you need to think twice. Day trading is not just meant for the chosen few. A while ago, people thought that the only people that were able to trade were those individuals working in big financial institutions, trading houses or brokerages. With the advent of the internet, trading has been opened up to all those that are interested in the activity. The exciting aspect of day trading is that it is a lucrative activity when one does it the right way. Regardless, we can't overlook the fact that it is often challenging for new investors in the market.

There is a huge misconception about day trading. Most people think that day trading is just like gambling. Due to this misconception, they end up giving up on their efforts to begin day trading. New investors in day trading business should understand that day trading is not similar to gambling in any way. So, the last thing you should be worried about is losing your money to unpredictable statistics. It is, however, understandable to get confused while engaging in day trading. There are endless swarms of financial transactions occurring within a day. This leaves men and women wondering how they can keep up. Day trading relies heavily on steady financial indicators which help in buying and selling of stocks, future contracts, currencies and stock options. The process is as simple as it sounds with some little technicalities you ought to comprehend.

One of the main reasons why day trading is not gambling is that it depends on facts and figures. With gambling, players rely on available odds to place their bets. However, day traders depend on past facts and figures indicating the level of performance of targeted stocks before they can make a purchase. Consequently, as you can see day traders have a wealth of information that assists them in making sound decisions.

You should also comprehend that day traders often apply logic and reason to their decision-making process. This is not the same thing with gamblers. True gamblers could be swayed by their emotions to bet on a particular outcome. Day traders refrain from this by all means possible. If traders realize the possibility of a particular stock performing badly in the coming few days, they simply ignore such stocks. Successful day traders in the market simply apply logic and reason to their decision-making process.

Day traders also have a unique winning mentality completely different from gamblers. Gamblers are always out looking for ways to make money overnight. As for day traders, they believe that getting rich is a slow and gradual process. Ideally, the slow process gives traders an opportunity to master the art of profiting from their daily investments. Certainly, patience pays.

The idea of day trading might appear as overwhelming for a novice trader like you. Nevertheless, when you break down the process, you will realize that it is based on simple rules that are easy to comprehend. This day trading eBook will take you through the basic attributes of the subject. It will explain to you what you need to know to become a successful day trader. Besides this, the book will point out possible hazards associated with day trading. To ensure that you enjoy the cruise, we will first begin with day trading fundamentals as we move to more advanced topics. By the end of the book, you will be fully equipped to invest in day trading without fear of losing your money. This manual also aims to adopt a unique perspective into the subject by refraining from the complicated jargon and out of the blues theories of day trading. Some interesting topics to anticipate in the material include recommended tips to avoid psychological challenges of day trading, developing your personalized, powerful day trading system, tracking news to enhance your day to day profit potential among others.

Chapter 1: Understanding Day Trading

What is Day Trading?

As the name suggests, this is the act of trading in financial instruments all through the day. You have to contend with the changes in prices during the whole day, meaning you have to be ready for both gains and losses.

Example

At 9.00 am, you might buy 2,000 shares of eBay stock and when the price starts to rise due to certain news, you can trade the shares at 10 am when the shares have gone up by $1.

This means that you make roughly $2,000 minus commission. When you deduct a commission, say $20, you make a cool $1980 in just 1 hour.

You need to note that day trading is aimed to give you small returns on each trade rather than a huge fortune via a single trade.

Why is Day Trading the Ideal Way to Make Money?

There are various ways to make money, but one of the best ones so far is day trading. Here are a few reasons to support this concept:

1. Ideal for Everyone

Day trading doesn't require you to be of a certain race, education level or gender – as long as you have the motivation and some money to spare, you are ready to go. So, whether you have a Ph.D. or you dropped out of school, you can still make money out of it.

2. No Office Space, Inventory or Equipment

In addition to your smartphone and the computer, you don't need to hire office space or stock any inventory. You don't need to fret about monitoring expiration dates, shipping, spoiled goods, insurance or advertising your products.

3. You Can work alone

Once you have access to the internet, you can work alone. The only team members are the ones that relate directly to your job such as the broker.

4. Minimum Time Required

Whether you run your own business or you have a day job, you can get time to trade and make money from the venture. You can place trades for as short a period as an hour each week and then build it up gradually.

5. Low Capital Investment

To take part in day trading, you don't need to have a lot of capital. Here, we are talking of as little as $1,000 to start. The venture is not like buying real estate where you need loads of cash to get started.

6. Instant Returns

Do you remember when you could invest your money into a venture then wait for ages before you get the returns? Have you ever wished to stop the running investment, which at times doesn't give any returns at all? For day trading, you can get your results within seconds of placing a trade! You can buy and sell the security again and make money several times a day.

Even if you lose a trade, you have the capacity to recoup your losses by running another trade that you are sure will give you a profit.

7. Low Costs Incurred

When trading, you pay less than $10 per transaction, which means that with the right trading model, you can make more profit on each trade compared to other trading methods.

8. Easy to Learn

As you will see in this guide, day trading is easy to learn. You don't have to sit in a classroom for several years to master the ropes of this form of trading. Unlike other careers, you don't need many years of experience to be relevant to the industry. Anyone can also learn to be a successful trader.

Day Trading Participants

So, who can get involved in day trading? Just like there are many advantages to day trading, it also comes with many disadvantages. This means that you will definitely encounter losses. Every trader knows that losses are a component of the game, take it or leave it – it is a fact you cannot run away from.

Additionally, it needs a well-laid out plan. Traders that enjoy the biggest success are the ones that have a solid plan to back them. They have trading strategies as well as the discipline to help them stick to their plan. You might have the best plan in this world but unless you have discipline, the strategy won't be profitable at all. You need to have discipline in order to follow the system rigorously.

You need to have some knowledge about the market and know what to expect from your actions. Many traders have tried to make money out of day trading but have failed miserably. They have bought all the tools, but lack the necessary knowledge to be successful at trading. As for everything else, education improves the way a trader operates, whether aspiring or experienced.

The perfect day trader knows that they will not get successful only with a single trade. What you need is to be consistent. This means you need to come up with a solid strategy that gives you consistent profits, regardless of the losses. As you trade more, you need to learn and adapt your strategies to better trading.

You need to have the time to trade and learn.

The Mindset of the Day Trader

Willing to Play above the Line

The successful day trader knows and understands that they need to be responsible for any action they undertake in the trading. Rather than putting blame on anything and everything, try and be accountable for the actions and trading decisions you take.

Remember that every market is the same, only a lot of terrible trading decisions made by traders. If you find that the market you thought was great has become untradeable. Then you can change to a different market. Alternatively, you can adopt a different trading approach. As a trader, you have very many things that you can do to turn things around.

Have the Right Attitude

Trading can be easy and simple, or very tough depending on how you regard it. Along the path of trading, you encounter losses, but this doesn't mean you give up because each day isn't the same.

To succeed, focus on going after your goals and forget the negatives. It is vital that you stay positive always.

Are Honest

Things can happen when you trade on a daily basis. Did you trade emotionally this week? Did you go out of your strategy? Well, you need to be honest and stick to your plan and take the blame when you make decisions that didn't add to your goals.

High Levels of Commitment

Trading success doesn't come overnight – it needs you to be committed and put in a lot of effort each day. Many traders lose out on trades because they thought that they know everything about trading only for them to come up short. They got into the market with the mentality that they will use a "magic" system that does everything for them without having to commit their resources.

Trading is similar to any other line of work, you have to gain knowledge of a few fundamentals, apply them and then achieve experience before you improve your trade. Remember that learning is unending, and with constant learning, you end up with the right experience.

Day Trading Plan

Before you can start trading, you need to come up with a plan. A plan is essentially a set of rules that shape and define your day trading behavior. This includes but not limited to money management rules, coming up with financial goals, risk management techniques and the criteria that guide the opening and closing of positions.

Many people in everyday life start with a plan of sorts, which they stick to because they know that it, will make them achieve their goals. The plan you have is what determines success or failure, the trading plan comes in any form that works with you, but for all forms, it needs to be written down.

It is not like you need the plan to be a complicated set of pages, but it should at least be documented down. It should be detailed to give you points of references whenever you need them

You need to know that the plan you come up with will be specific to your niche. Many people try to buy a plan from another trader with total disregard to this point.

Why Do You Need a Trading Plan?

There are different reasons why you need to have a day trading plan. Entering the world of day trading can be tough for most people, say with the high competition and the many technical aspects to consider.

• Having a trading plan before you start to trade is much like having a blueprint before you start building your house. Would you start building without knowing what you desire? Day trading minus having a plan can be challenging.

• With a day trading plan in place, you get to treat the trading more like a business. Many of the successful traders knew that to run their business the right way requires a business plan.

• The business plan enables you to make quick decisions to leverage the benefits that arise in a fast-moving market.

• The manor advantage of having a day trading plan is that you get the opportunity to trade in an objective way, therefore, you place trades with greater confidence while eliminating emotional involvement.

• The rules in your plan will help you to overcome emotional and psychology responses to trades. One of the signs of a successful day trader is that they have an undaunted attitude regardless of the direction the market will take at the end of the day. Human emotions such as greed, hope and fear can be a huge impediment to trading leading to losses.

Chapter 2: Common Characteristics of a Day Trader

Professional day traders are those who do this type of trading for a living. While other forms of trading can sometimes be done as a hobby or a gambling high, day trading is often not included here. Day traders are typically well-established in the field and they have spent quite a bit of time working in the stock market. This makes them equipped to recognize changes in the market and to learn the trends of various industries, helping them to pick out the right trades to make money with day trading. Some of the prerequisites to day trading include:

• Experience and some knowledge about the marketplace.

If you don't have a good understanding of the market and its fundamentals, you will most likely lose money.

• Enough money to start.

You need to have some savings or other money that you can put towards day trading. Make sure this is money that you can afford to lose. This helps to keep some emotions out of the trade and can help you make smarter choices with your trades. Often, you will need a large amount of capital is needed to capitalize effectively in this type of trading.

• A good strategy.

A trader needs to have a way to beat out the rest of the market. There are many strategies (some of which we will talk about later) that can help you with day trading. Each of them can be effective; you just need to pick the one you feel comfortable with.

• Discipline.

All day traders need to have some discipline. If you aren't able to stick with your chosen strategy, then you will lose money. Success is virtually impossible without some discipline.

Using Day Trading to Make a Living

There are two divisions when it comes to professional day traders. The first one is those who work alone. The second is those who work for a larger company. Most traders who do this kind of trading for a living will work for a large company. This is helpful because these individuals will have access to a lot of tools that an individual trader only dreams about. These can include some expensive analytical software, a lot of leverage and capital to start, and a direct line to the trading desk. These types of traders are looking for profits that are easy and ones that can be made looking at news events and arbitrage opportunities.

This doesn't mean that an individual trader isn't able to do day trading on their own. They may not have a trading desk of their own but they may have some strong ties to a brokerage and some other resources. If you are an individual trader, you won't be able to compete with some of the larger companies, but there is still a niche market that you can join.

If you wish to use day trading as a method to make a living, then there are a few things that are required to make this happen. These include:

• Some sort of access to a trading desk.

This tool is often reserved for those traders who work for a larger company or those who will manage a lot of money. The dealing desk provides these traders with the ability to do trades instantaneously which is very important to the success of day trading. If you don't work for a large financial organization, you may need to discuss with your broker what options are available for you here.

• Several news sources.

The news is going to provide you with the information you need to pick the best trades in day trading. You need to be one of the first to know when something big is about to happen. Then, you can jump in the market in the beginning and get a good price. Once everyone else catches onto the news, you can sell your security and make a profit.

Having at least three or four news sources that you look through each day can help you figure out the right trades to make.

• Analytical software.

When it comes to day trading, analytical software is going to be so critical. It may be a bit expensive when you get started but it is a necessity for most day traders. For those who are working on swing trades or technical indicators, you will rely more on this software than the news. Some of the features that you will want to find in your software include:

• Pattern recognition that is automatic.

This means that when you work with the trading program, you want it to identify technical indicators such as channels and flags. You may even want some complex indicators such as the Elliot Wave patterns.

• Neural and genetic applications.

These are programs that will utilize genetic and neural networks to help make your trading systems better. They are good at making more accurate predictions when you are trying to figure out where the price is going to move in the future.

• Broker integration.

Some software applications are going to make it possible to interface directly with the brokerage. This makes it easier for an individual trader to do an automatic execution of trades. Not only does this help you to get into and out of the markets at the right time, but it can also take some of the emotions out of the game.

• Backtesting.

Backtesting can be useful because it allows a trader to practice a bit. You will take your strategy and test out how it would have worked if you used it in the past. This is not always completely accurate, especially if the market turns a different way. But in some cases, it can give you an idea of how your current strategy will work in the market by basing the information on historical data.

When these tools are combined, they can provide a trader with a big edge over others in the marketplace. And when it comes to working with day trading, they are really important. Without them, many traders without the right experience can lose money in the market.

How Is Day Trading Different Than Swing Trading and from Long-Term Investing

If you have ever researched other forms of investing or have done any other forms, then you will find that day trading can be a little bit different than the others. There are a lot of different types of investing that you can do and understanding how they are all different can make a difference in how you approach this kind of trading.

First, there is day trading. Day trading is when you get into the market at some point during the day. It can be any time that you want but most people choose to enter after the first five minutes are done to avoid any issues with the volatility in the market. Then, at some point during the day, you will exit the market. This can happen a few minutes after you do the initial trade, it could take a few hours, or you will wait until the end of the day. How long you stay in the market will depend on how well it is doing and the strategy that you picked.

Day traders will look at short-term charts to figure out moving averages, resistance and support lines, and to make better decisions in investing. Outside of news that happens right within a company, they will not concern themselves with how the company will work in the future or what changes will happen beyond that day.

The biggest thing here is that you enter the market and exit the market all in the same day. You should never leave your position open overnight. Doing this results in different strategies and is actually swing trading. Swing trading is similar to day trading but it takes place over a longer period of time. Most swing traders will last between two days and two weeks. This gives you a little more time to prepare and make your moves but it is still pretty fast paced. You will hold the position overnight but if your profits don't happen within a few weeks, you need to exit.

Swing traders are going to focus their energy on preparing for a big trend. You are going to look at the news and other indicators to figure out the best times to enter the market because a big change is about to happen with a company within the next few weeks. These traders enter before others catch on to the change, getting the stock for a good price. Then, when everyone else is alerted to the news and rushes to purchase the stock, the swing trader can sell their stock and make a huge profit as well.

Then there is long-term investing. This is often what is done for those who want to earn an income from quarterly dividends in the company they invest in, or those who are looking to invest to help out with their retirement. They are looking for the long-term trend of a company and hoping that it goes up over many years rather than over a few hours and they don't really look at the daily ups and downs for a company.

With long-term investing, you are going to need to look more at the fundamentals of the company, rather than the technical parts. This helps you to determine whether the company is secure, if they will continue on the path they currently follow, or if there are any concerns that you need to focus on before investing in that company.

Day trading is very different from some of the other forms of investing but it is still very appealing to different investors. It provides an opportunity to really learn about the market and to make money quickly, as long as you are able to use the system in the proper manner.

Chapter 3: Day Trading Pros And Cons

While the above makes day trading sound relatively straightforward, the truth of the matter is that it has a variety of pros and cons that means it is not for everyone. Take a look at the following list to determine if there isn't another type of trading that is better suited to your goals.

- Pros

• Large profit margins: For those who do it right, day trading can be a very profitable career path with profits that are greater and more reliable than just about any other type of securities trading.

• Work for yourself: Many of the most successful day traders are self-employed which means they don't have to answer to anyone, they can make their own hours and set their own profit goals.

• Always exciting: Dealing with the shortest market timeframes means that day traders typically see more action than any other type of security trader. You will have the opportunity to pit your wits against the market as well as your competition each and every day. Those who are natural thrill seekers will also appreciate the adrenaline rush that comes from rapid-fire trading and pulling a big win from the grip of defeat.

• No degree required: As opposed to many other financial jobs, a perfectly successful day trader can be completely self-taught. As long as you are willing to put in the time and energy to learn the skills you need, you can be a success with no expensive courses or degree required. Everything you need to learn can be found, for free, online.

• Tax write off: As self-employed individuals, day traders can write off plenty of their expenses when it comes time to pay taxes. Hardware, software, even home office space can all be written off by those who work from home.

- Cons

• High commission costs: Due to the fact that they make so many trades each day, day traders need to be careful of which brokerage they use as commission costs can easily eat into profits if they aren't careful.

• Extreme loss potential: Statistically, day trading is the most difficult type of securities trading to make a profit from on a reliable basis. A vast majority of day traders see nothing but losses for at least the first month they start day trading on a regular basis and more than 60 percent wash out before they ever turn a profit.

• High barrier to entry: Freelance day traders are typically competing against a wide variety of professional organizations that have a trade capital reserve of millions of dollars. This means that in order to have a chance of entering the market successfully they need to have a sizeable bankroll on hand, as taking out loans to fund your day trading dreams is never recommended. Additionally, you are going to need to factor in hardware and software costs as well as commissions, brokerage fees, live price quotes and more which will all add up much more quickly than with other types of trading due to the high volume of trades that are made on a regular basis. Outside of the financial concerns, many brokerages will not allow you to day trade until you have proven yourself competent at trading on a smaller scale beforehand.

• Self-employed: While there are certainly benefits to being your own boss, there are also plenty of drawbacks as well. This includes a lack of a retirement plan as well as health insurance, no assurance of a steady paycheck or a corporate infrastructure to help you out in any way. Additionally, you will need to keep in mind the relative isolation that comes with working by yourself with no one to lend a hand when you need it or to prevent you from browsing social media instead of working. Additionally, you will likely need to give up your steady paycheck before you start making reliable money day trading so that you can focus on it completely and get to where you need to be.

Knowing what leads to follow

Premarket movers: If the market hasn't opened yet, then the price of a given stock is always going to be subject to change. Nevertheless, it is still going to be an excellent place to start when it comes to deciding if a given stock is going to be worth trading on a certain day. The first thing you will need to be on the lookout for is those with a greater than average amount of volatility for the previous 30 days before checking to determine if the price at close lower or higher than average as well.

Social media: These days, there are just as many social media groups dedicated to the ins and outs of the markets as there are more official sources, and many of them manage to get the early scoop on the comings and goings of the market quite frequently. This, in turn, will make it easier for you to determine how the market is likely going to move before it has a chance to get started which will make it easier for you to get in on the ground floor of beneficial changes.

Earnings Calendar: A surefire way to see an increase in volatility is when earnings are reported. You are never going to want to jump on an assumed trend before they are released but shortly thereafter the trade gates will be thrown wide open.

Characteristics of a successful trader

Proper expectations: When it comes to honing your trader's mindset, perhaps the most important thing you can do is understand the results you are likely to experience. Having realistic expectations will allow you to respond appropriately both in times of failure as well as success. Specifically, this means you are going to want to banish thoughts of major success in a short period of time. This, in turn, will make it easier for you to prevent negative thoughts from creeping in throughout the day and causing you to take risks you otherwise would not take.

Additionally, it is important to be aware of what your emotional triggers while trading are likely to be. As everyone's triggers are different, the best way to understand your own is to keep a trading journal. In this journal, you are going to want to keep track of all of your trades, both successful and unsuccessful. You are going to want to note the date of each trade, the specifics surrounding it, the emotions you felt at the time, whether or not it was successful and why.

This exercise will not only help you to be aware of the emotions you are likely to experience in the future, it will help you understand why they appear in the first place. Emotions are the enemy of good trades and the best way to outpace your enemy is to know them inside and out.

For many traders, the strongest emotional triggers occur because they believe that correctly executing on a plan should lead to success 100 percent of the time. This stems from a misunderstanding of what considering a plan successful actually means. When it comes to options trading, a successful plan is one that hovers around a 60 percent success rate. This means that the plan is extremely likely to turn a profit in the long run but a full 40 percent of the time it is used it will end in failure.

Early riser: While trading in New York doesn't begin until 9:30 am, the most successful traders use the early morning hours to catch up on the international markets so they have a broader idea of what the day is likely to bring. Having a strong macro view is crucial to taking advantage of micro changes. The Western economy is strongly influenced by global markets and understanding one makes it easier to predict the other.

Dedicated: Common wisdom says that in order to truly master something complex, such as day trading, you need to put in 10,000 hours of practice time. This equates to 8 hours a day, for roughly 3.5 years. This is to say that becoming an expert day trader is more akin to a marathon, not a race.

Lifelong learner: The best day traders aren't the ones that are confident they've heard and seen it all before, they are the ones that understand that new and improved techniques are always coming along. Being constantly on the lookout for the newest advances in theory and strategy is what separates the true pros from the rank and file amateurs who will never be able to trade full time. The markets change every single day which means that even analysis from 7 days ago can be hopelessly out of date. Don't curtail your earnings potential make the choice to maximize it every day; remember, if you want to earn, you have to learn.

Patient: Once you have determined an ideal trade, you must be able to wait for the perfect moment when the price reaches your predetermined exit or entry point. You must follow your predetermined system and if the market doesn't reach your numbers you have to have the patience to move on to the next ideal trade. Chasing potential gains by altering your exit or entry points on the fly will rarely lead to success, it is best to wait for the ideal time to buy or sell instead.

Objective: It is important to approach each trade from a completely objective free standpoint. Regardless of any external factors, the best trades are those that are made based on a reliable system; it is as simple as that. If you listen to external sources, then you are letting other systems dictate your movements instead of your own. Evaluate each trade on its own merits and trust yourself to make the right decision.

Trading Discipline: As a new trader it can be tempting to pursue certain trades just because they "feel right." This, in turn, leads to a scattershot approach which will hurt your success in the long run. When it comes to making trades stick with these hard and fast rules.

• Focus on absolute truth: The only truth any asset has is its price in the moment. Don't get attached to trades good or bad, attachment will keep you from selling when all the signs point to sell.

• Follow the logic: If you choose an asset based on a proven strategy which says it is a good choice, you made the right choice even if the trade goes poorly. It is important to have a strategy and execute on it every time regardless of individual results (assuming it is a sound strategy, to begin with). Eventually, the odds will even out in your favor.

- Always know the odds: Prior to every trade, it is important to determine the level of risk versus the potential reward. Everyone's percentages are different depending on personal circumstance, know your risk/reward levels and never exceed them.

- Doing nothing can be the right choice: It can be easy to get into the habit of trading every day even if your current trades are still performing at acceptable levels. If it isn't broken, don't worry about fixing it.

- Let go of greed and fear: While trading, the two emotions you will encounter most are fear and greed. You will be afraid to make a trade and you will lose money because you waited. You will be greedy and hold on to something for too long and in so doing lose money. The sooner you learn that raw data is all you can trust when it comes to trading effectively the better.

- There are no shortcuts to success: There is no surefire system or program that will guarantee results, you can only improve as a trader by trading regularly, keep a tally on your results, seeing where you need to improve and working to improve in those areas. It is called practice, and it does make perfect.

The Benefits of Day Trading

There are traders who recommend against getting into day trading. They worry that day trading is too risky, too fast-paced, and that it is too hard to actually make any money with this form of trading. There are actually a lot of benefits that come from day trading as long as you know how to read the charts and how to do an accurate trade. Some of the benefits that you can get from day trading include the following:

- Day trading can eliminate some of your overnight risks.

Depending on how the market does, there can be fluctuations that go between five and ten percent. The stock that is making a higher low and a higher high, and which even closed that day at a new high, has the ability to open up the next day at a low level. In one night, if things don't go right, you could wipe out all of your profit. And this all happens when you are sleeping! This doesn't happen with day trading because all of the trades happen and finish in one day. Political developments, disasters, and news are not going to disturb you. You can finish the trade and then go to bed without worries.

- You can use leverage.

Many brokers will offer you several times more than your capital margin. This provides you with more opportunities to control more investment than is available. If you are careful with your trading, this is a good way to multiply the profits that you can make. Leveraging is not usually recommended for beginners because it could result in you losing a ton of money as well but it is something to consider.

- Gives you a better chance to learn about the market.

Because you are doing a lot of trades each day, this is a great way to help you test out some trading patterns and learn more about the market.

- It can be done at home.

You can technically do day trading from home around your own time. You would just enter and exit the trades around your other obligations. Or, if you get good enough at this type of trading, you would just work this when you want to and can get all the profits in your free time.

- The satisfaction of the different challenges.

Many traders find that the continuous changes in the market can give them a feeling of accomplishment. It is an adrenaline surge that they enjoy and that keeps them working on this kind of market.

The Negatives of Day Trading

While many traders are able to make a good income with day trading, it is not the best for every trader. Some traders may want to work more with a long-term option. They may be interested in something that has a little less risk. Or maybe they aren't interested in being hooked to the computer and worrying about all the little shifts that occur in the market and how it affects their current trade. Some of the disadvantages that show up for some traders who are considering day trading include:

• During market hours, this trading takes a lot of intense focus.

If you have a lot of trouble focusing for a long period of time, or there are obligations that make it hard for you to do this, day trading can be frustrating. Day trading includes a lot of staying on your toes to figure out when the best setups are going to come along.

• You may miss out on some overnight gaps.

As many professional traders will tell you, there is a lot of money being left on the table when it comes to those overnight gaps.

• The market may move a lot but that doesn't mean your trade will move.

This happens often when we talk about day trading. This depends on how often the market makes a big move and then you either have a loss or barely break even. As a new trader, this may not make much sense, but it does matter with day trader.

• The market hours aren't the best for everyone.

Those who live on the east coast may have no problem with the hours but if you live in any of the other time zones, it can sometimes be difficult and inconvenient to trade in the U.S. markets. Some like this time difference though because they can get up early in the morning and get some good deals. Either way, you will have to watch the market and make the times work for wherever you are.

• There are a lot of opportunities for the trader to over trade.

Overtrading, either taking too many opportunities than you can handle or trading too big, is often something that happens with day trading. If you lack some self-discipline, remember there are always other trading methods to go with. The extra buying power that comes with this method of trading can give you a loose leash. If you have a lot of issues with staying disciplined, the temptation to overtrade could lead to your demise and a lot of lost money.

- You may spend too much on trading costs and commissions.

This can end up costing you a lot of money if you are not careful. Any time that you shorten up the timeframe you are working with which can come up with day trading, those commissions can sometimes cause issues.

- You will need more software than other forms of trading.

A good day trader will have some charting software, a scanner, and a broker to help them evaluate all the different choices that they can pick from. You can do day trading without this but it becomes a lot harder when you do.

Day trading can be a great way for you to make money but there are some situations where it is not the best option for you. Explore how day trading works and some of the positives and negatives before determining if it is the right trading method for you.

The Basics of Day Trading in Futures

Many people think of day trading as working with stocks. While this is one option you can choose, some people like to work with other options, such as futures. Futures can be effective because there isn't going to be a restriction on shorting when you work in this market.

First, let's look at what futures are. Futures are going to be financial contracts that will obligate a buyer to purchase their asset or a seller to sell their asset. This can be a physical commodity or a financial instrument. They differ from options, that is, you have to buy and sell these if you enter the contract, while an option will let you choose if you want to buy or sell. The contracts for these futures will detail the quality and the quality of the asset you are purchasing, and you simply need to set up the time limit of these to be for one day, rather than over a few weeks or months, or even years, to make it day trading.

While a day trading strategy for futures will often have many components and can be analyzed for how profitable it is in may ways, it is often going to be ranked based on the win rate, or the reward to risk ratio. The win rate is how many trades won based off all the trades that you did. So if you win 55 out of 100 trades, your win rate is 55 percent. As a day trader, having a win rate above 50 percent is pretty good. You can also work with the reward to risk ratio. This helps you determine how much risk you have to take to get a certain profit.

Since you are required to purchase or sell the future based on the contract you pick, it is important to pick a day that has a lot of volatility. This ensures that the price has time to go the direction that you want before you have to sell off. If the market isn't moving much, you may have to sell before you can make a good profit, or purchase when the price is too high.

Day trading with the Forex market

Another market that you can consider using when it comes to a day trading strategy is to trade in the Forex market. The forex market is a global decentralized market that allows traders to invest in currencies. This includes all the aspects of buying, selling, or even exchanging currencies at a determined price. In terms of the volume of trading, it is the largest market in the world. The main participants in this market will be international banks. But some individual investors choose to get into the market and make money as well.

Trading in the forex market is a great way to take advantage of changes in one economy over another. You will find that it is very similar to trading stocks and other options, but with day trading, you will really need to pay attention to the market and watch when the price of one currency goes up or down. Some of the basic guidelines that you can follow when you choose to day trade with forex will include:

• Trade just when the US and London markets are open. You may only want to trade for a few hours a day, usually when the two markets open. This helps you to not get worn out and make mistakes.

• When you trade, work with the one minute charts. This helps you to keep up with the small changes.

• Only trade in the same direction of the trend. You won't be in the market long enough to worry about anything else.

• Wait for a pullback. This pullback needs to stall out at some point or show some signs that the price is starting to move back in the trending direction. This must happen before it reaches a major prior swing low.

• When you see a pullback, your price needs to consolidate, which means that it must move sideways for at least two bars. Then you can purchase a breakout that is above the high price of this consolidation. This can take some patience because it may not stall the whole way and you may have to wait for some time.

• Put in those targets and stop losses. These ensure that you are going to get the best results and won't lose too much money.

• If you hear that there is a major news event that is about to happen, you need to leave all of your positions a minimum of two minutes ahead of that. You don't want to trade again until after the news is released, so even cancel all pending orders when you hear of new news or when you plan to be away from the computer. This makes sure that you aren't going to stay in the market and get on the wrong side of consumer sentiment about the news.

• Create a good day trading routine. This keeps you on track and can help you avoid some mistakes in the process.

There are some investors who want to trade in other markets, but usually until you become more accustomed to working in day trading, it is best to stay with the US market. This way, it is easier for you to get the news that you need to make informed decisions.

Day trading with crypto currencies

A newer option you can choose for day trading is crypto currencies. These crypto currencies are taking over the world and many people are starting to notice. There are thousands of these currencies available and they offer security, anonymity, and a great way to make a profit if you use them the right way. And since their volatility is high, you can easily make a lot of profit in a short amount of time.

You have to be careful with this kind of investing though. There are no regulations on the currency and they aren't available on the stock market. They also have a lot of ups and downs with them so it is also easy to lose your money quickly if you aren't careful. You really need to do your due diligence here because with so many options of crypto currencies to work with, many of them are not strong, and many can be fakes. And since these currencies aren't regulated, you won't be able to get anyone to help you out if you pick the wrong type of currency.

Now, if you take the right precautions and are willing to watch the market to protect your money, crypto currencies can be perfect for earning money with day trading. In fact, after seeing the crash of Bit coin in January 2018 after the currency reached almost $20,000 and then crashed to under $10,000 in a few days, investing in these currencies over the long-term isn't the best. But the high volatility in these currencies make them perfect to join into the crypto currency market, stay in for a few hours, and then get out and make a good profit in the process.

If you do decide to invest in crypto currencies, make sure that you take some time to research charts and the history of that currency. There won't be any reports from the SEC for you to read through and make informed decisions. Instead, you need to look online, read the charts, and learn the patterns of the currency on your own. But a smart investor who is willing to take the time and learn can make a big profit in no time.

Some crypto currencies, such as Bit coin, are more established and can be great options to go with. Others are newer and you may need to do your research on as well. You also need to check the amount of variation that comes with the market. If you are only going to make a few dollars on a trade, it may not be worth your time. Just like with your broker, these crypto currency markets are going to charge you to exchange your fiat money with the crypto currency of your choice.

Chapter 4: Types of Day Trading

An important part of day trading is understanding the different options available to you and which will best suit the time you have available, your finances, and even your interests. Although all day trading activities seek to make a profit by purchasing stocks and selling them at a higher price on the same day; there are several different types of day trading:

Futures

This is one of the most popular options for many day traders and an excellent place for a beginner to start. On the stock market, a futures contract is one which has been created between two parties one of whom agrees to sell a certain amount of stock to the other in the future, but the price is fixed at the time of the contract. These contracts can then be bought and sold on the market as different speculators decide whether they can make a profit on the maturity value of the futures contract.

Day trading in futures simply means that you are focusing on the future contracts and looking to buy and sell any which will turn you a profit within a day. Future trading is a good guide regarding the market and where it is going in general. This makes it easier to trade in as they produce a more reliable picture of prices than many other types of trading.

Options

There are two types of options; 'puts' and 'calls'. A stock option is a contract between two people. As the buyer of the option, you will purchase the right to buy shares from the other party at a set price, within a set timeframe. A call means you have the right to buy at the agreed price, whilst a put means you have the right to sell.

If you are trading on the stock market, this can be very beneficial. You can purchase the option at a low price and wait for the price to rise. Once the price has risen, you can then complete the purchase by actually buying the shares and selling them immediately to someone else, making a profit along the way.

Day traders will often deal with the options, buying the right to buy shares from someone and selling the option on to someone else. In principle, this is the same as dealing in options on the stock market, but the risk is lower as you do not expend any funds until you find a buyer. The option to buy is yours, but this does not mean you have to!

Currencies

If you have ever been abroad and needed to change your money into another currency, you must already understand that currency rates vary daily. This volatility allows people to trade on two currencies of their choice and make a profit.

In simple terms, you seek to purchase a set amount of a certain currency, for example, 200 US$. This may cost you 150 GBP. If you then wish to change your funds back, the exchange rate may have moved. This is a result of market demand; the more popular a currency is; or the more the resources of a country are needed, the better the rate of exchange will be. If the US market improves, you may need to pay 175 GBP to get the same 200 US$. If you have already purchased the currency, you will be able to change it back and make yourself a 25 GBP profit, less any transaction charges.

Day trading in currencies works on exactly the same principles; you will be able to trade online with any currency around the world and potentially make good profits. Of course, every trade involves you being a buyer and a seller, which does increase the risk.

Stocks

The first thing most people think of when considering the stock market is shares. Purchasing shares and holding them for the long term to make money from both increased value and dividends is a tactic employed very successfully by many investors.

It is also possible to day trade in the same way; however, your window of opportunity is much smaller! You should purchase those shares that are at the bottom of their fall or already on the way up. This should allow you to purchase some and then sell them again later the same day for a profit.

To be successful day trading in stocks, you will need to keep a close eye on the stock market and which companies are performing well. The best ones to invest in are those which normally do well but have had a blip thanks to an unforeseen but fixable event. These shares will usually dip and then re-climb throughout the day.

Arbitrage

By now, you should be aware that there are many different markets and it is possible for you to trade in any of these. It is also possible for you to trade in more than one market at the same time and make money doing so. This type of trading involves locating a product which is selling for less in one market than it is another. Once you have located the product, you purchase as many as you can in one market and sell them all instantly in the other market. The risk is minimal as you hold the stock for only a few moments. The price difference simply needs to be enough to provide a small profit after allowing for the costs involved in the trade.

There are usually very small windows of opportunity available to make profits trading this way. The process of arbitrage actually helps to consolidate the prices across the different markets; it is an excellent way of keeping trading fair! At the same time, it provides the opportunity to create a decent profit, depending on how much you can afford to invest in the process.

Momentum Trading

Big companies can be hugely affected by news in either the wider economy or by events which happen inside their business, but the information is publically available. There is no hard and fast rule as to how the market will react to any specific news. It is essential to wait until you see the market movement.

Once you are certain that the share price is climbing or dropping, you will be able to purchase your shares. Only buy as the share price climbs and the momentum builds. Generally, events like this will hit a share price and then naturally rebalance later in the day. This is why it is essential to monitor the trend and sell when it starts to go back down.

Always buy in a rising (Bull) market and sell in a decreasing market (bearish). It is best to set yourself a target price, which should be at a level that will allow you to make a reasonable profit after allowing for the transactions costs involved in buying and selling.

Swing trading

It is natural for the price of any commodity to change during the course of a day. Swing trading attempts to profit from these movements of prices. You need to identify the products or stocks which are moving throughout each day. At some point, they will go from higher to lower and then back again. Operating as a swing trader means buying at the low end of the swing and waiting for it to go back to the top end of the swing, all within the space of a day. It is important to note that you do not need to buy and sell at the top and bottom of the swing, as long as the difference between the two prices will give you a profit and cover costs. Even a product which has very small swings can be a good investment; small consistent profits can quickly mount up.

No matter which option you choose to trade in, it is important to always have a professional approach and to treat your day trading as a business. There are many people who have attempted day trading and lost substantial funds as they have not been prepared or had the right approach. Any trading on the stock market requires research, patience, and an understanding of how the stock market works. The more you know about your chosen market sector, the better you will be able to predict the up and down movements and purchase the right day trading option for the occasion. It is possible to day trade in all the different options listed above. It is even possible to day trade as part of a larger investment strategy. The key is to be prepared!

No matter which type or types of trading you commit to, you should always sell and consolidate your position at the end of the day. The prices listed on the market can change dramatically overnight, and you will have little ability to recover your capital, you will only be able to watch your funds disappearing and hope they recover to some extent in the morning. This is not a good position to be in and emphasizes that you have not prepared properly.

Chapter 5: Creating the Right Plan for You

In addition to creating trading rules for yourself, you are going to want to focus on creating a personalized trading plan to help further minimize the effect that emotions have on the trades you make. In order to get started creating this plan, the first thing you are going to want to do is to learn as much about the types of markets you are interested in trading in as possible. Don't rush through this step in order to get to trading as quickly as possible either, it is important that you really take the time to understand the inner-workings of your chosen markets.

This way, once you do start trading you can do so from a perspective of one who is truly up to speed in regard to what is going on. This knowledge will also help you overcome both greed and fear so it is a useful tool in its own right in addition to preparing you to make better decisions in the long-term.

Understand your personal trading style: In order to create a reliable trading plan, the first thing you are going to want to do is to take some time to consider your personal strengths and weaknesses when it comes to trading. Day trading is the stock market investment big leagues and if you are going to trade with the big boys you need to know that you can handle the competition. As such, if you are not confident in your abilities then you will want to stick to lower-risk trades and strategies while if you are more confident then you can work with greater amounts of leverage and riskier trades all around.

When doing your self-assessment, it is important to keep in mind that it is not a test and that you are not trying to impress anyone. If you end up overestimating your capabilities the only person you will end up hurting is yourself. With that in mind, you will want to go over every facet of your trading experience with a fine-toothed comb in order to ensure that you aren't giving yourself more credit than you really deserve. While looking at yourself so closely might feel uncomfortable, you should really try and look at what you bring to the trading table and, if you do so, you will come out stronger because of it.

Additionally, it is important to consider how well you can control your emotions, even when things aren't going your way and how likely you are to stick to your plan once you have created it. After all, it doesn't matter how airtight your plan is if you don't have the emotional and mental fortitude to stick with it once things stop going your way. If you feel as though you are naturally in control of yourself at all times then you will already be well on your way to improving your overall trade results. If not, you will need to favor strategies that allow you to take your emotional nature into account. Failing to do so is simply asking for trouble.

Consider your goals: It will also be important to consider your goals when it comes to day trading as these can easily affect the ultimate strategy that you choose to pursue. This could be something safe, such as keeping your initial trading capital intact no matter what, or it could be something with a greater amount of risk and potential reward. The specifics themselves don't matter, what matters is that you take the time to clearly identify your plan and then stick with it once it has been instigated. When choosing your goals, keep in mind that your trades don't exist in a vacuum, be sure to accurately consider any external factors when in the planning stage.

Understand your relationship to risk: There is no surefire way to determine what the right amount of risk is for you to take on with each individual trade. Some people are going to be able to sleep soundly at night after making risky trades and others are going to end up being awake all night when any trade is left on the table. There is nothing inherently wrong with either of those positions, as long as you determine which side of the coin you fall on before you start making trades. Taking trades that are outside of your comfort level, even if someone you trust says it's a good idea, will only lead to trouble in the long run as you will essentially be trying to jam a square peg into a round hole.

Once you have determined what your ideal level of trading risk is going to be, you will then be able to turn to the task of choosing the types of strategies that will best support your natural proclivities. Choosing strategies that work with your natural feelings about risk, rather than against them will ultimately allow you to make more effective decisions as a trader overall.

Once you know your acceptable level of risk as well as the strategies you feel comfortable using, you will then be able to accurately determine how frequently you are going to need to trade to make the amount of money you are hoping for while trading. Keep in mind that the higher your tolerance for risk, the more you are going to need to trade in a given month in order to hit your target in order to take into account the greater number of failed trades you are going to experience. This means when determining your tolerance for risk you are also going to need to consider how comfortable you are with micromanaging your trades as opposed to setting them up and letting them run.

Choose your moments carefully: Prior to entering into any short-term trade, it is extremely important that you know when you are going to be willing to walk away either because you have made an adequate profit or because you can't realistically afford to go any further into the red. The urge to stay in wring every last cent out of a successful trade is natural in relatively new traders and is often misleading as overtime it is likely to cause you to lose out much more than you will ever gain.

When it comes to choosing the right exit points you will always want to focus on the limits of your tolerance for risk and avoid changing the exit point once the trade has started, no matter what. On the other hand, when it comes to choosing profitable entry points you will never want to make a move on a trade that doesn't mesh with your own natural tolerance for risk. It doesn't matter how good of a deal a trade might be if it falls outside the level of risk that you are comfortable with then you will never be able to act on it as effectively as possible.

Once you know the types of trades you are looking for in general then you will be able to look into various types of strategies that support those types of trades. There are countless different strategies available, as long as your plan is profitable then you should easily be able to find one that fits your plan like a glove.

Asses your plan: Once you have a plan in place, the next thing you are going to want to do is to try it out for approximately one month in order to determine if it is effective or not. If it is, then great, otherwise you will need to rework it until it is successful approximately 60 percent of the time. While that might sound low, the fact of the matter is that no trading plan is going to be 100 percent reliable and a plan that is 60 percent reliable is going to be enough to turn a profit in the long run. Once you have given your plan some time to work, it is important to stick with it, assuming it is successful in the general sense, even when you have a streak of bad luck. Changing your plan too often is only going to lead to confusing results that will make it difficult for you to determine if you are on the right track. Stick with a single plan and you are likely to see much better results overall.

Work to minimize risk: To ensure that you minimize risk, it is important to keep in mind that the best strategies are those that focus on either high positive risk value or high negative risk value, there is little value in betting on the middle ground. Remember, some trades are always going to end up being more profitable than others in specific scenarios, you just need to have the patience and the foresight to know what's coming before it gets here. With that being said, however, it is important to always keep in mind that statistical projections cannot actually tell the future which means that any analysis that is done is strictly hypothetical. Never invest more money into a particular trade, no matter how reliable it seems, than you can ultimately afford to lose.

When it comes to making trades in groups, or combining them in other ways, it is important to consider the net risk of the entire trade instead of focusing on the specific risk likelihoods of parts of the whole. This will make it easier for you to determine the most profitable way to move forward at any juncture because it makes the risk/reward split much easier to analyze. Remember, there are multiple different types of risk which means that understanding what each means for your specific trade is crucial to covering all your bases and making success options trades on a reliable basis.

Improving your plan: When it comes to improving your trading plan, the first thing you are going to need to do is to make plenty of trades and ensure that each and every one is properly recorded with screenshots, targets, stop loss levels and any other notes you need to make sure you can easily recall the specifics of each as needed. The emphasis of the importance of screenshots to this process cannot be overstated as it can easily show the results of specific actions in certain market settings.

Once you get in the habit of doing this, let your records build for a few weeks before starting to analyze them in an effort to make your trading plan more effective and specifically tailored to experiences you have already had. It is important to not get ahead of yourself, however, as two trades that ended poorly or three that ended successfully, do not necessarily indicate a trend. Don't be in too much of a rush to find patterns, however, as this can just as easily work to your disadvantage as well. Instead, it is best to analyze your data and find clear examples of mistakes you made or positive trends you might otherwise have missed.

Additional ways to assess your performance and improve your trading plan include determining the percentage of your trades that are winners as opposed to those that are losers. While a high percentage of winners is nice, it is meaningless on its own. You will also need to determine how much you gain on average when you have a positive trade as opposed to how much you typically lose once a trade has gone south. Only by determining your own specifics for each of these metrics can you really start to determine where or if your trading plan needs to change. If your numbers seem acceptable then it is likely just your inexperience that is keeping you from achieving the type of success you are looking for, keep up the good work.

Chapter 6: How To Manage Your Risks

If you want to be successful at day trading, there are three things that you need to have. You need to have a sound psychology that can handle the stress of this trading style, a set of trading strategies that will help you make good decisions, and a good plan to help you manage your risk. If you are missing out on one of these parts, your whole program will fail, and you will not make money with day trading.

As a beginner, it is easy to focus only on the trading strategy that you are using. While the trading strategy is pretty important, it leaves you without the other three components that are just as important. Just because you have picked out a good strategy to work with does not mean you have the right self-discipline to stick with that strategy or to wait the market out long enough, and this could be the reason that you are failing, regardless of the strategy that you pick.

For this chapter, we will talk about risk management. There will be plenty of time for the strategies that you can use later, but for now, we need to learn some of the rules that you must follow to manage your risk. Of course, any strategy that you pick will have times when they will lead to a bad trade. The market does not always behave the way that it should or that we expect. But when you learn to manage your risk, you will not lose out as much money as you would just jumping into the market.

The first thing that you should do to manage your risks is to draw a line in the sand or have an exit point when you will decide it is time to get out of the trade. Pride can be hard to swallow for a lot of people, and they may find that it is hard to admit defeat or that they were wrong about a trade. But holding onto that trade will simply lead you to losing more money and will make the mistake bigger than before. You need to learn when to cut your losses and then walk away.

There will be times when the trade goes against you. This happens to beginners as well as to those who have been in the market for a long time. When the trade starts to go against you, it is time to exit. It is common in day trading for the unexpected to happen all of the time because there are such big fluctuations in the market from one moment to another. It may be hard to admit the defeat, but remember that there are always other trades that you can do on other days.

Your main job in day trading is to make money. If you are holding onto a position that is going against you just because you want to be able to prove that a prediction you made was right, then you are a bad trader. Your job here is not to always be right; it is to make money.

Another thing that you should do to minimize your risks is to always follow the plans and rules of your chosen strategy. This will be really easy when the trade is going well, and you are making money. But when you are in the middle of a bad trade, you may be tempted to go against those rules. This may seem like a good idea at the time, but it can end up costing you a lot of money. Following the rules of your strategy may make you lose a bit of money, but it is much easier to lose a little and get back into the game later than to end up with a big loss. It is better to take some of those quick losses, get out of the trade, and then come back to it all later on.

Next, you need to make sure that you are finding low-risk entries that can provide you with a high potential reward. These can be risky still, but they pose a lot less risk than you will find with other stocks that you choose. The best setup is when you find an opportunity that will provide you with a trade that has a very little risk. For example, risking $100 to make $300 is a good setup, but if you are risking $100 to make $10, you are in the wrong trade. Most expert traders are not going to work on trades that have a ratio of less than 2 to 1 for profit-to-loss.

What this means is that if you purchase $1000 of stock and you are risking $100 on that stock, it is important that you sell that stock for a minimum of $1200 to make it worth your time and to decrease the risk. Of course, it may not always work out that way, and you may need to accept a loss, such as when the stock goes down to $900, but there should at least be the potential to make $1200. If the potential is only to make $1100 on the stocks, the profit-to-loss ratio is too low, and you should not risk it.

On some days, you are not going to be able to find a stock that has the right profit-to-loss ratio. That is fine. It is much better to stay out of the market for a day than to trade on a stock that does not provide the requirements that you need. You can enter the market later on, on another day or two down the line, knowing that you did not risk your money in the process. With the 2 to 1 ratio, you will be in a good position. Remember that there are still going to be times when you are wrong, or the market goes the opposite way than it should. If you stick with this ratio or better, you can still be wrong 40 percent of the time and make money from day trading.

The three questions to ask

Whenever you decide to purchase a stock on a trading platform, you are risking some of your money. Even stocks that fit into the ratio that we talked about before can run into some issues, and you have to realize that you are risking your money each time that you do this. However, there are some steps that you can take to manage this risk. The questions that you should ask yourself before any of your chosen trades include:

• Am I trading with the right stock: the first step of risk management is to work with the right stock? If you pick out the wrong stock, it does not matter what tools or platform you are using, you will end up losing. You need to make sure that you are avoiding stocks that do not have any movement, penny stocks that can be highly manipulated, ones that have a small trading volume, and those that are already being traded heavily by institutional traders and computers.

• What share size should I work with: the next question is to decide how many shares you should purchase. This will depend on how much money you have available and your daily goals. If you only want to hit a target of $1000 each day, then you will need to purchase more than 20 shares in most cases. If you do not have enough money in your account for this kind of target, then it is time to lower the daily goal.

• What is my stop loss: this is basically the amount that you are comfortable with losing if the market goes south. The most that you should never risk more than two percent of the equity in your account. This means if you have an account that holds $10,000, you should not risk over $200. This means that you may not make as much of a return on investment on your trades, but also helps you to keep most of your money in your account.

The three-step risk management plan

Step 1: the first step that you should take is to determine the absolute maximum dollar risk that you will take for the trade you are planning. It is recommended that as a beginner, you should never risk more than 2 percent of the equity in your account, but you can choose to go up and down from this number based on how much money you have and how much you are willing to risk. You need to have this amount calculated before you even start trading for the day.

Step 2: the second step is to estimate the maximum risk per share that you will take, the strategy stop loss, from your entry. We will learn more how to do this later because you will have a different stop loss based on the strategy that you choose.

Step 3: take the number from step 1 and divide it by the number you got from step two. This will give you the maximum number of shares that you can trade each time. Do not go about this level, or you are increasing your risk too much.

Let's take a look at how this would work. Let's say that you will get some stocks and you have $40,000 in your account. If you stick with the rule of only using 2 percent, then you would limit your risk to $800. We will be conservative for this trade as beginners and only risk 1 percent of the account, or $400. Now we have finished step one.

As you are monitoring the stock, you see that a situation is developing where you would use the VWAP Strategy (more on this later on) to get the best results. So you decide to sell the short stock when it reaches $50, and you want to cover them at $48.80, with a stop loss at $50.40. This means that you will be risking about $0.40 per share. This will be step 2.

Now we are moving on to step three. We will calculate our share size by dividing the numbers in step 1 and step 2, so we can find the maximum size that we can trade. For this example, we would be able to purchase a maximum of 1000 shares.

Now, with the money that you have in your account, you may not have the right buying power to get the shares at $50. So, you would choose to purchase fewer shares, such as 500 shares to get started with. With the strategies that we have talked about, you are never allowed to risk over 2 percent, but you can always be conservative and riskless.

Making sure you can handle the stress

And finally, to manage your risk, you need to make sure that you are actually able to handle the stress that comes from day trading. This is a stressful job. You are not able to just place your money on the market and then walk away from it, checking in on occasion. Rather, you need to be watching your stock the whole day. All those little fluctuations up and down can have a big impact on your potential earnings, and this can add a lot of stress to your day.

If you do not have the time to devote to this, at least on the days that you decide to trade, then this is not the right investment option for you. If you have trouble dealing with stress or you already have enough stress in your life, then day trading is not right for you. If you are not good at making decisions at the last minute and you let your emotions take over, then day trading is not for you.

Day trading can be a great investment option for you to work with, but you need to make sure that you are managing your risks and keeping them as small as possible. With the right strategy and risk management plan in place, even when you lose a little bit of money on an occasional bad trade, you will still be able to make a lot of money with day trading.

Chapter 7: The Tools and Platforms You Need

Like with any business you choose to go with, there will be some tools that you need to become a successful day trader. The most important tools that you will need are an order execution platform. And, if you are not already part of a trading community, you may need to have a stock scanner that will help you to find the best real-time setups that will make you money. Let's take a look seat what kinds of tools you need and how you can pick out the ones that are right for you.

Choosing your broker

When you first get started with day trading, especially when you are a beginner, you should find a good broker. Your broker will be the one who offers you advice on which stocks to go with and they will help you to execute these orders at a good price and at the right time. There are a lot of different brokers out there, and picking out the right one will ensure that you will get the best results with your day trading. Pick out the wrong broker, and you will be disappointed.

The first decision that you need to make is the type of broker that you want to work with. There are some benefits to each one, and it often depends on how much you would like to spend, how much work you want the broker to do for you, and what features you would like them to offer to you. Some of the different types of brokers that you can choose from include:

• Interactive Brokers: The first type of broker that you can choose is an interactive broker. These brokers are pretty inexpensive and can cause you $1 or less per trade. When you are purchasing 1000 shares or more, this is a pretty good price compared to almost $5 or more that other brokers will charge you. Depending on where you live, they may also work with you without having to hold a large sum of money in the account ahead of time, making them easier to work with.

• SureTrader: This is a good option for those who are international traders and those who fall below the $25,000 minimum that is a rule for U.S. residents who want to day trade. They will charge a bit more for commission though so be careful when you are choosing one. These companies will often charge you almost $10 for completing one buy and one sell. But if you are from the United States, and you do not have $25,000 available to trade, this is one of the best options to go with because they do allow you to open an account for as low as $500.

Of course, there are many other types of brokers available. Some will offer you just advice to help you get started if you just want to do the work on your own. This can save you money, but remember that you are not going to get a lot of help in the process. On the other hand, you can also choose from a full-service broker who will not only offer you some advice but will be able to help complete the trades for you. It often depends on what you are looking for when it comes to your broker before you start.

One of the benefits of choosing a broker is that they will give you some leverage, about three to six times the leverage. This means that you may only put in $30,000 into the market, but you will have $120,000 in buying power (which means that you have a leverage of 4:1). This leverage is known as margin, and with many brokers, you can trade on the margin. This can help you out if you are short on money to get started, but you have to be responsible. Buying on the margin is easy, but it is also very easy to lose all of your money as well. The margin is good because it can give you the opportunity to purchase more than you could on your own, but it adds in more risk, and you may have to pay back more money than you can afford.

If you are using this leverage and then losing money, the broker will issue out a margin call. This is a serious warning, and it is best if you just avoid getting this at all. When you receive a margin call, it means that your loss is so much that it equals the original money that is in the account. If you do not add in some more money to the account, you will get a freeze on your account.

This is just one of the features that your broker may be able to offer you. Some will be able to offer platforms that are unique and will put you ahead of the rest of the game. Some will have different types of stocks that you can invest in and so on. It is a good idea to not only look at the fees that a particular broker is asking for their services, but also take a look at the different features and services that you would be able to get with them. You may be tempted to go with a cheaper option, but when you see all of the special features that another one offers compared to that cheaper option, it may be a better idea to spend a bit more.

Trading platform

As a day trader, you need to be able to complete your trades quickly, or you will not be successful. If you are working with a broker who does not use the right software or platforms, you may not get out of your trades fast enough, and you could end up losing money or missing out on a big profit. You do not want to be in the middle of a trade and see a big spike and then not be able to make changes or sell the stock because your platform is not the best.

There are many different trading platforms that you can work with. One option is known as DAS Trader, and it is really efficient when it comes to all of the things you need to do as a day trader. They have a helpful support team, and they are located near the NASDAQ data centers, so you are right in the middle of the market. There are many brokers that offer this platform when you are opening your account, while others will have their own platform.

The best thing that you can do is check out and see how much you like the platform before you get started. Many brokers will have a trial run or a way to give the platform a try so that you can get familiar with how the buttons work and everything ahead of time. You may find that you like one platform better than another based on your own personal preferences. But no matter which platform you choose to go with, make sure that you are going with one that is quick, efficient, does not experience a lot of downtimes and will make your day trading easier than ever.

Real-time market data

With day trading, you need to be able to look at real-time data during the day. You do not get the benefit of waiting a few days or weeks for this data to come out because you need to enter and exit a trade in a short period of time, sometimes within a few minutes of each other. There are some tools available for this, but remember that you will need to pay a fee for this, either to the platform you are using or to your broker.

Some people do not like the idea of spending more money. They are already paying for their broker and some of the fees that are needed for their platform, and adding more seems like a waste. But depending on the market that you wish to trade in, you will find that having this real-time data will help you out a bit. It will help you to see what is going on in your market and can make it easier to adjust your trades, get out of the market when it is needed, and even to increase your profits.

Joining a trading community

Day trading can be a very difficult thing to work on, and as a beginner, you may feel emotionally drained when you are done. And you are likely to have a lot of questions along the way. It is a good idea to join a community of traders and talk to others who are in the same boat, asking questions as needed, to get the hang of things. It is normal to have some questions when starting out and joining one of these communities can make a big difference in how much you can do with day trading and whether or not you will be successful in the long run.

Having the right tools will make a big difference in how successful you can be with day trading. A good broker will be able to provide you with good advice and can even help to quickly execute the trades for you. The right platform will ensure that you will be able to make the trades right when you need to. The right real-time scanner will let you catch some of the trends and keep up with how your stocks are doing. And a good community will be able to help answer any and all of the questions that you have along the way. Make sure that you have some of these tools, and you will be set to go.

Chapter 8: Technical Analysis

When working with technical analysis you are always going to want to remember that it functions because of the belief that the way the price of a given trade has moved in the past is going to be an equally reliable metric for determining what it is likely to do again in the future. Regardless of which market you choose to focus on, you'll find that there is always more technical data available than you will ever be able to realistically parse without quite a significant amount of help. Luckily, you won't be sifting through the data all on your own, and you will have numerous technical tools including things such as charts, trends, and indicators to help you push your success rates to new heights.

While some of the methods you will be asked to apply might seem arcane at first, the fact of the matter is that all you are essentially doing is looking to determine future trends along with their relative strengths. This, in turn, is crucial to your long-term success and will make each of your trades more reliable practically every single time.

Understand core assumptions: Technical analysis is all about measuring the relative value of a particular trade or underlying asset by using available tools to find otherwise invisible patterns that, ideally, few other people have currently noticed. When it comes to using technical analysis properly you are going to always need to assume three things are true. First and foremost, the market ultimately discounts everything; second, trends will always be an adequate predictor of price and third, history is bound to repeat itself when given enough time to do so.

Technical analysis believes that the current price of the underlying asset in question is the only metric that matters when it comes to looking into the current state of things outside of the market, specifically because everything else is already automatically factored in when the current price is set as it is. As such, to accurately use this type of analysis all you need to know is the current price of the potential trade in question as well as the greater economic climate as a whole.

Understanding trend: To use technical analysis properly it is important to understand how trends work and how best to analyze them. In forex, a trend is any noticeable grouping of pricing data that points in either a negative or positive direction which indicates the direction the market will likely move in a predetermined period of time. Trends that are very easy to pick out are said to be strong which those that are more difficult to see are said to be weak.

While strong trends speak for themselves, it is important to be cautious around weak trends as it can be easy to mistake random market movement for a weak trend that doesn't exist. This is more difficult than it might initially seem as forex prices have been known to clump together in a suspicious fashion or to move around erratically in ways that trends typically signify. In order to minimize the likelihood of misidentifying a trend, the best thing to do is to focus on identifying the highest highs along with the lowest lows and discounting those data points in the middle. Remember, every data point doesn't need to line up perfectly to prove the existence of a specific trend when it comes to technical analysis majority rules.

Positive trends, also known as uptrends, and negative trends, also known as reversals, aren't the only types of trend that you need to be on the lookout for. Horizontal trends also exist and they are the definition of middle of the road. Specifically, a trend is said to be horizontal when all the moves that it makes are negated thanks to a series of opposite and equal moves in the other direction.

Trends can be of any length and the longer a trend is the stronger it is. If you come across a trend that seems to cut off shortly, it is important to look at the underlying price movement over a larger period of time to ensure that you just aren't missing the forest for the trees. The best way to ensure that you have accurately determined the type of trend you are looking at is to make it a habit to consult charts that cover both short and longer time spans as well.

Once you have properly consulted your charts, you will then want to generate a trendline as a means of determining if your assumptions are correct. For uptrends, you will need to connect the points of all the lowest prices over the given timeframe which a negative trend will see you connecting the points of the highest prices on the timeframe. If the trendline ultimately ends up above nearly all of the data points then it is a line of resistance, which is the point that price is likely to start receiving pushback when it is climbing. If the line is below most of the data points then it is the support line which means the price is unlikely to drop below it. This will not indicate how long a given trend is likely to continue, just where it is likely to end up when it peters out.

Finally, once you have come across a specific trend you will need to determine the channel it is a part of which is crucial when it comes to determining the right time to act on the information you have chosen. To do so, you will need to first determine both the price floor as well as the price ceiling of the currency in question. This will make it easier for you to determine if the trend is neutral, negative or positive as it should clearly be one of the 3. You will then want to trace what is known as a channel between the pair of lines for as long as it takes for the price to break through it. The breaking point is going to be your time to make a move as it indicates the period when significant negative or positive movement is going to occur.

Indicators to watch

Moving average convergence divergence indicator: The moving average convergence divergence (MACD) indicator is a type of oscillating indicator that generally moves between the centerline and zero. If the MACD value is high, then this indicates the related stock is close to being overbought and if the value is low then the stock is in danger of being oversold.

MACD charts are generally based on a combination of multiple exponential moving averages (EMAs). These averages can be based on any timeframe, though the most common is the 12-26-9 chart. This chart is typically broken into multiple parts, the first of which is the 26-day and 12-day chart. Using an EMA that is slower or fast allows you to more accurately gauge the current momentum level for the trend you are currently keeping an eye on.

If the 12-day EMA, the fast of the pair, ends up being above the 26-day EMA then you can safely assume that the underlying stock is on an uptrend while the reverse will also be the case. If the 12-day EMA increases at a rate that is greater than the 26-day EMA then the uptrend is generally going to be even more pronounced. IF the 12-day EMA starts to move closer to the 26-day then you can accurately assume that it is slowing down which means the momentum of the trade is going to fade. This, in turn, means you should expect the uptrend to end shortly.

The MACD puts these EMAs to use by considering the difference between them and then plotting it out. If the 26-day and the 12-day end up being the same then the MACD will equal out to 0. If the 12-day ends up ends up at a higher point than the 26-day then the MACD will end up being positive, otherwise, it will be negative. The larger the difference between them, the further the MACD line will fall from zero if the result is negative, or from the center line if the result is positive.

While the MACD doesn't provide all that much more detail when compared to the standard moving average, its value increases dramatically when it is used in conjunction with the 9-day EMA as well. The 9-day EMA differs from the other EMAs in that it is based on the MACD line as opposed to the stock price. As a result, this EMA then smooths out the MACD line to make its results more useful overall.

On certain occasions, you will also find a use for the MACD histogram which visualizes the difference between the MACD line and the 9-day EMA line. If the MACD line cross through the 9-day EMA line at a point higher than 0, then the upcoming trend is likely to be bearish, otherwise it is likely to be bullish. If the charted histogram generates a number of descending peaks, then this will be known as a negative divergence, while a positive divergence forms in the opposite way.

If a negative divergence occurs, then it is a strong sign that any positive trends that are currently in place will be reversing sooner than later. This will remain true in all scenarios, even if the underlying stock price seems to be in the midst of a very strong positive trend. The same is true in the opposite sense for positive divergence and negative trends. These signals can become somewhat muddy when the price trades at the range for a prolonged period of time which is why it is important to always use multiple indicators to avoid seeing false signals.

Consolidation indicators: Consolidation is the term used in technical analysis as a means to describe the fact that the price of a given stock tends to stick to the same pattern, regardless of the trading level that you view it from. More practically speaking, consolidation can be thought of as the period of indecisiveness that is guaranteed to come to an end after the price moves outside the existing pattern. These types of consolidation are surprisingly common and can be found across any price chart at nearly any timeframe.

When they do appear, technical traders tend to use them as a means of finding levels of resistance and support so that they can ensure the buying and selling decisions they make are as informed as possible. These levels are generated by the underlying asset and the fact that it is likely to vary a predetermined amount over a given period of time. This means that once the price moves outside either the pre-existing resistance or support level, volatility will increase dramatically as a result.

This volatile period is when smart traders will jump in to make serious profits in a short period of time. Furthermore, many technical traders believe that the breakout does occur on the side of the resistance then the price is going to typically continue to move upward which means you would want to go long in response. However, if the breakout instead occurs so that it is on par with the existing support then it is likely that the price is going to continue to decrease which means you will want to take a short position instead.

Both pennants and flags are signs of retracements or deviations from the existing trend that eventually become visible in the short term if viewed in comparison to the existing trend. Retracements rarely lead to breakouts occurring in either direction, but the underlying asset likely won't be following the dominant trend in the first place so this shouldn't be much of an issue.

Chapter 9: Day Trading Techniques

Day traders use a multitude of techniques to try and make a profit. Every single one of them is very useful to the average trader though it must be said that flexibility is the most successful strategy a day trader can use. This chapter seeks to outline some of these trading techniques and their relevance to day trading. Some of these techniques involve shorting stocks, instead of buying them, adding an increased risk factor to the transaction. Below are four of the most basic day trading techniques used by day traders everywhere.

1. Trend Following

Trend following is not a strategy used in day trading alone but in all forms of financial trading. It can be defined as the trading in securities and stocks not due to their market value, but due to the particular trends that have been affecting the market values over a set period of time.

In conventional trading circles, the trends can be followed over a period of days or weeks or even months to discern what the best investment would be. With day trading, however, the trend is followed over a much shorter term, a couple of hours at most.

A market 'trend' is the ability for a market price to move over time, whether it moves up or down. Most traders who practice trend following will study the market and wait for a trend to establish itself, and then depending on the nature of the trend, either buy or sell stocks on the market. Trend following is a good way to trade because it allows you the flexibility to decide for yourself whether the investment you are making is sound before diving into it.

Trends are affected by a number of different things, some of which prolong the current trend. For instance, some traders look for information that will confirm their beliefs about a particular trend. Confirmation bias like this has the power to keep the trend going, as once confirmation is found, the investor will apply it to that situation.

Therefore, if the trend is negative, the investor will sell his shares to avoid losses, continuing the negative trend for that particular stock listing.

Factors that have to be considered when trend following include, but are not limited to:

a) Price: This is by far the most important thing when it comes to trend following. Though other indicators may be used to forecast price fluctuations, only the actual price will give you an idea of how you need to interact with the market.

b) Risk Control: Though completely eliminating losses is an impossible task, minimizing your losses should be paramount.

c) Money Management: It ties into risk control and involves the decision of how much to invest in a trend. Too much and you risk losing more than you should, too little and you may not reap any benefits at all.

d) Rules: Stick to the rules you laid out for yourself, trend following should be systematic.

e) Diversity: Recent research has shown that diversifying the assets that you follow is vital to professional trend followers.

2. News Playing

News playing is as the name suggests, playing the stock market depending on the news you have received for a particular security or stock on that market. If reports received state that a particular stock is doing well, then that would be a good reason to buy into it. Successful day traders can keep their emotions in check while news playing, as they know that emotion should not affect their final decision.

Once a particular news item has been released, it is important as a day trader to look at how this news is affecting the stock prices. As most news will be internally circulated before being released to the public, there may be a slight change in the share price just before any news is released. If there is a negative appreciation of the share price just before a news item is released, then it means that you need to sell your stock to avoid making losses. With day traders, it is said what is perceived is their reality while conventional traders rely more on logic.

For instance, when AOL and Time Warner joined forces just before the Dot-com bubble burst in the early 2000s, a day trader's profit margins were very high. Long-term investors at the time were not so lucky, as the merger seemed to have success written all over it, but three years down the road, the investment proved to be a disaster. In the short term, the perception of the success of the merger was enough to guarantee a profit margin for day traders, but with the passage of time, that opinion proved to be illogical, and hence the long-term investors suffered losses.

3. Range Trading

Range trading or Range-bound trading is a type of trade where a certain asset or stock is watched over a specified period of time. These stocks will have been rising and falling in value in an almost predictable pattern, with maximum and minimum values that can be pinpointed with relative ease and accuracy. The difference between the maximum and minimum values is called the 'range' or 'swing' of the stock value.

Range trading is often thought of in relation to trend following, but that is not the case, as with range trading unless there is an unexpected breakout in the range, the trend remains the same. Once a stock's range has been broken, however, it is safe to assume that the trend that broke it be it a breakout (an increase in share price) or a breakdown (a decrease in share price), will continue for some time.

The best way to make money with range trading is to buy the stock when it's on its way back up the channel from its lowest point on the scale, then sell the shares when they reach the peak price. Some range traders even go to the extent of short-selling certain stocks as they know that a higher profit margin will be possible.

Mathematical algorithms in computer programs are often used to eliminate the human emotional factors that may affect a day trader's decisions and are often written to give the trader buy and sell signals for selected securities.

Range trading is quite risky for all traders, long term investors and day traders alike, as the risk of incurring losses increases when trading in a range. A sideways price movement in the share price may also mean that no gains can be made on your investment. Worst of all, if there is an unexpected breakdown in the share prices, losses to you as a day trader can be enormous.

4. Scalping

Scalping is also referred to as spread trading and can be defined as the exploitation of the bid-ask spread by trading in securities rapidly over a very short period of time, usually minutes or even seconds. The theory most traders use when scalping is that stocks that make small increments in stock price are easier to catch than big ones.

Most scalpers will make between 10 and a couple of hundred transactions a day in the hope that they will make a profit. Scalpers have been compared to market makers as they help to maintain the liquidity of the market.

There are certain universal principles that all scalpers that trade on the markets are aware of. These are

a) The lower your exposure, the lower your risk

With scalpers holding stocks for just a few minutes on average, their exposure to those stocks is substantially reduced. This diminished time period means that there is a lesser chance of a scalper gaining huge losses due to changes in the stock price.

b) Small moves are easier to catch

The stock price on any given item is mostly determined by the same old demand and supply principle that drives prices in other industries. In stock trading, this is not usually affected on a day to day basis, but over time. Scalpers, rather than look for big moves with large spreads that rarely occur, look for small moves with small spreads that happen more often, increasing their chances of profiting from a sale.

c) Large Volume means Low Profits

Most scalpers will agree that this practice is not suitable for the large capital traders who are looking to move large volumes of shares at one go. This is because the profit margin that is gained from trading in shares with low spread values is negligible to the large investor. For this reason, scalping is more suited to investors who are trying to move smaller volumes more often to gain the biggest profit margins.

d) Spreads are bonuses as well as costs

As most securities exchanges worldwide operate on a bid and ask based system, and then it must be noted that the spreads between these two (the bid and the ask) do become important when you are scalping. When a trade is executed at market prices, it is important to know which side of the fence you are on. If you are the buyer, you will end up incurring costs in terms of the spread, whereas if you are the seller, you make a profit on your sale because of the spread. Sometimes holding on you your shares for a few minutes can increase their value enough that you make significant profits, but not many scalpers are willing to queue (hold on to their shares) preferring to take the small profit margin and repeat the cycle, rather than risk that margin on a 3 minute window that may yield no fruit.

These are just a few of the basic techniques used by day traders and as you can tell all of them come with their own risks and benefits. Traditional long-term investors would avoid some of these strategies as the risks seem too big to take on while the benefits would be minimal. Good day traders, on the other hand, understand that it is for precisely this reason that massive profits can be made, and, therefore, the rewards greatly outweigh the risks.

Chapter 10: Day Trading Strategies

Now that you have a sound idea of what the best day trading techniques are, you can begin to strategize so that you can make a substantial reward from all of your efforts. The ultimate goal for any day trader is to make a sizeable profit, and in order to fulfill this goal, it is necessary to control a big amount of capital.

Day traders understand that when working towards making this profit, speed and timing are everything. This is because they are focused on finding and making use of the minutest movements in stocks which have high liquidity or index. Without the right strategy, they are unlikely to succeed. A retail day trader can try out the following strategies: -

Strategy for Entry

It is not every stock on the market that is suitable for a day trader. There are certain criteria that make some stocks more viable than others. A day trader will evaluate a stock based on two variables. The first is the liquidity of the stock. This primarily looks at the pricing of the stock, and the ease with which a trader can enter or exit this stock. The best stock for day trading will have a tight spread, as well as a low spillage.

The second variable that a day trader will evaluate is the volatility of a stock. The mention of volatility explains movement, and in day trading, it refers to the movement in price. When evaluating volatility, the day trader takes into consideration the price range that is expected for the day. This could have two significant results; it could lead to heightened profits or significant losses.

Once liquidity and volatility have been assessed, and the stock has been identified as being appropriate for trading, the next step is to look into the best way to identify entry points. For this, there are two tools that come in handy.

Candlestick Charts

These charts are highly popular and are essential for any day trader. They display the prices for specific securities on a daily basis. By analyzing a candlestick chart, it is possible to know the day's highest and lowest prices, as well as the opening and closing price.

In addition to this, the shape of the candle in the candlestick chart reveals more information. The section which is wide is referred to as the 'real body'. It is within this section that one can analyze the closing price in relation to the opening price, by assessing whether it was higher or lower. This is denoted by specific colors. When the stock closes at a price that is lower, the candle will be black or red in color. However, when it closes at a price that is higher, the candle will be white or green in color.

The shadow of the candle in this chart also tells a story. It explains the highs and lows for the day, and this can then be compared to the opening and closing prices. So in the final analysis, just the shape of the candle will vary based on all the movements taking place in a day's trade. This type of chart provides a straightforward analysis of pricing for the day.

Level II Quotes/ECN

When a gambler goes to the races, they receive a thrill by watching everything unfolding live, right before their eyes. There is an equivalent for this in day trading, and this is referred to as Level II. A trader who is using this strategy is watching the trades being executed live, right before their eyes. This is based on quotes from specific market makers. As everything unfolds, rapid decisions can be made to ensure that any small gain is capitalized on – in real time.

ECN stands for Electronic Communication Network. This is an automated system which allows traders from different locations to trade with each other easily. It works by matching buy and sell orders. This system is great for a day trader who operates as an individual because by using an ECN, the trader can actually connect directly with a major brokerage. This cuts down on fees for a middleman, and also saves time, allowing for faster and more profitable trades. The added advantage of an ECN is that trading extends beyond the typical market hours, and includes after-hours trading.

In addition to these two tools, there is a chart that can prove handy when reading information for data trading. Simply being able to understand the information that is available can go a long way in creating a foundation for success.

Discerning the information from day trading transactions would be a challenge if there was no mechanism in place to make it possible. All the information from day trading is arranged in different types of trading charts. By using these trading charts, a day trader is able to keep an eye on the markets that they are trading on, and this makes it easier to make informed decisions about when they should be making their trades. It also allows them to monitor the movements on the market on a consistent basis.

There is a range of different trading charts that are available. These trading charts will all provide you with similar information, and that includes the prices that are currently being traded. Of all the available options, there are three which are referred to with heightened regularity. Candlestick charts have been discussed above. The other two are explained in this section.

Bar Charts

These are basic, easy to read charts that contain all the significant and standard trading information. This information includes but is not limited to the opening prices, closing prices, and so on. The layout of the chart makes it very simple to read, and even easier to interpret. There are certain key bits of information that are also included in the bar chart. The first of these is the open, which is an indication of the first price that was traded during the bar. Next, there is the high, which indicates the highest price that was trading during the bar. The third piece of information is the low, which gives an idea of the lowest price that was traded during the bar. Finally, there is the close, which details the final price that was traded during the bar.

By reading these prices on the charts, one can make some conclusions about the bar. First, the inclusion of the open and close reveal whether the bar managed to close in a position that was higher than when it opened. Then, the inclusion of the high and low reveal whether the bar fell within a particular range and that range can then be analyzed. This range would be the distance that can be seen between the high bar and the low bar.

Line Charts

Of the three types of charts listed here, these are the least popular. When looking at day trading charts as a whole, these are highly popular. In the same way that the other mentioned charts contain all the significant trading information, the same applies to the line charts. However, these charts have the added advantage (or disadvantage depending on your perspective) of only being supported by using charting software.

The charts that are used during trading will all have their own unique way of displaying information, and this means that they also have different ways that they should be read. This, in turn, will affect how they are interpreted by traders.

There is software available that makes the process of reading these charts much easier for the day trader. This software is also used for creating charts. Almost all day-trading brokerages today will use charting software.

Defining Stop Losses

The main aim of a trader has been established as making a profit. Day trading is exciting and thrilling. When a day trader is going through the rapid motions of the day, it is quite possible to get caught up in the speed of things and make decisions that may cost money, are reckless, or have not been given due consideration.

To stay on the safe side, the trader needs to set up a stop loss order. This will help to guide the sales of the security, as a stop loss order is one where a broker is instructed to make a sale on a security once it has attained a particular price. The aim of putting this in place is to limit the loss that an investor may incur. When an investor is unable to place a significant focus on their daily trading, a stop order comes in handy as it helps to keep the day's trading within a certain control.

A day trader who trades on margin will be the one most likely to define a stop loss. Once a day trader has determined the amount that they are willing to lose, a physical stop-loss order can be put into place. If for any reason a trader's entry criteria appear to be violated, then a mental stop loss set at a specific point will be triggered.

All traders need to be careful to ensure that they do not lose everything that they have in their portfolio in a day, simply because they were operating without a clear head or plan. It is imperative that a day trader should set a maximum loss for each day, especially one that will not break the bank. It should also be the type of loss that will not cripple you mentally and financially. No matter what may be happening during the day, when you reach your maximum loss, stop trading. It may be tempting to try making up any loss in the last trades of the day, but efforts like these in the last minute will usually backfire.

Practice, Perfect, Patch-up

If you are under the impression that the moment you start day trading, having mastered the techniques mentioned earlier, you will make a significant profit, you are highly mistaken. Have you ever seen a child learning how to ride a bike? They get on it, are given a little push, and before long, they fall off. They will fall off several times before they finally get it right. The only way that they can develop the skill for riding the bike is through practice.

When you go into day trading, it will be some time before you can make your profit. You will spend some time losing before things begin to pick up. You need to keep practicing the techniques in order to get things right.

Following practice, you can begin to perfect. At this point, you are improving the methodology that you have employed for beating the odds. Patching things up requires an evaluation of a person's personality, to assess whether everyone is on the same page. In day trading, the focus should be on creating a strategy for a good trade, rather than looking at the profit as the only result of business.

Chapter 11: Common Mistakes With Day Trading

As a beginner, you have a large learning curve that you need to work with before you are able to profit on a consistent basis with options. It may sound pretty simple from some of the examples that we have provided so far, but you do need to take the time to learn as much about options as possible and to get the most out of your investment.

Learning what mistakes other beginners make and how to avoid them can make all the difference in how successful you can be with options trading. Let's take a look at some of the common mistakes that happen with options and how you can avoid them to earn as much as possible.

Buying Options without Hedging

This is a big mistake that a lot of beginners will make, and it can end up costing you a lot of money. Buying a naked option means that you are purchasing an option without any protective trades in order to cover your investment, in case it goes the wrong way and ends up hurting your profits. It is really hard to predict how the stock is going to move over the short-term, and there are going to be times when you are not accurate. If you keep on purchasing naked options, you are basically hoping to get lucky each time, and you are hoping that you will not lose more than you gain over the long term.

In order to make a good profit after purchasing a naked option, there are a few things that need to happening including:

• The trader needs to be able to predict the direction the stock will move accurately.

• The movement of that stock needs to be fast enough so that the position of the trader can close before its gains get overrun with time-decay.

• The rise of the options premium price needs to compensate for any drops that may happen from the time that the option was purchased.

• The trader needs to be able to exit the trade before the reversal of the stock price happens.

As you can see, there are going to be times when it is a challenge for all of these things to occur and fall into place. This is why it is common for naked-options traders to lose money, even if they were able to correctly guess the way the stock would move. There are still many traders who assume that if they keep following the same steps, they will end up with good results in the long run. The best way to make an income from options is to never purchase a naked option, unless you are doing it to hedge another position, because the risk is too big.

Underestimating Your Time-Decay

Another mistake that you may make as a beginner is that you underestimate your time-decay. This can be one of the worst parts of being an options trade if you are not able to exit the trade fast enough.

As a call options buyer, you may notice that sometimes, even when the price of the stock is increasing on a daily basis, the call option's price is not rising or falling. As a put options buyer, you can sometimes notice that your put options price is not increasing, even if there is a fall in the price of your stock. This can be a bit confusing to someone who is just starting out as an options trader.

These problems are going to occur in the market when the increase or the decrease of the stock's price is just not going at a rate fast enough to outstrip the rate at which the options time-value is eroding each day. This means that with the strategy that you employ for trading, you should have some method of minimizing or at least countering the effect of time-decay. There are even some strategies that will use time-decay in their favor to ensure that the trader gets a profitable trade.

Buying an Option with High Volatility

Another mistake that you can make is to purchase options in a time of high volatility. During these times, option premiums will often get overpriced, and if you purchase an option, you could still lose. There are times when the stock can move sharply in line with what you are expecting; a large drop in the implied volatility could make the price of the option fall quite a bit, resulting in you losing money.

You want to make sure that you are purchasing options when the price is not so volatile. This will ensure that the price of the option or the stock doesn't go down further than you were expecting and that you will not pay too much for your options premium.

Not Cutting Out On Your Losses When Needed

A good saying that you should stick with when it comes to options trading is to cut your losses short and let the winners run. Even those who have been working in options trading will find that one of their trades has gone badly on occasion. The difference between the novice and a more experienced trader is that the experienced trader knows when they have lost and when they should get out of the market. Many beginners keep holding on to trades that are losing in the hopes that these options will bounce back and they will make money.

The issue with this is that when they hold onto these options, they hold onto them a lot longer and lose a big chunk of their capital. Rather than losing a lot of money, an experienced trader will know when to admit that they were wrong, and they will pull out early when the losses are low. Then they will still have some capital leftover in order to spend on another options contract.

Being able to cut your losses in time is crucial, especially if you are working with a directional strategy and you make the wrong call. The most practical thing that you can do is exit your losing position once you notice that it is moving against your expectations and it erodes over two to three percent of the total capital you want to earn.

If you are someone who likes to use the spread-based strategies, the losses that you have will always be more limited when you have made a wrong call. However, no matter what strategy you are using, once you notice that your trade is not going to profit you well, it is time to cut off the losses and choose to reinvest in a different position that can bring in better profits.

Adding Too Many Eggs into the Same Basket

As mentioned, there are going to be times when you will make a bad trade, no matter how much time you have spent in the options market. An experienced trader knows that they should never place all of their bets on a single trade. If you do this and the trade goes wrong, it means that you are going to lose a lot of your capital all in one place.

Professional traders know that they should spread out their risks across at least a few different trades so they won't lose all their money in one place. It is best to keep no more than five percent of your available capital in one trade in order to keep things safe. So, if you have $10,000 to invest total, it is best to never enter into a trade where you will risk losing over $500 if things go wrong. If you are able to follow this practice, it will ensure that losing on occasion is something that can happen without you eating up all of your cash reserves. If you do not follow this advice, you can easily place too much of your money into one trade, and if it goes wrong, you will lose a lot of your capital.

Using Brokers Who Charge Too Much

When you are investing, it is important to cut down your costs as much as possible. While you do not want to be cheap and cut corners, there are some brokers who will charge way more for their services compared to others. You can choose to go with another option that will save you some money.

You do need to do some research ahead of time. Just because a broker charges less doesn't mean that they are the best ones for you. There are many brokers who will charge you a fair rate, but make sure that you look at some of the features that each one offers and pick one that will provide you with the results that you would like.

As you can see, there are some common mistakes that beginners can make that will cost them a lot of money on options trading. But when you learn about these mistakes and how to avoid them, you have a head start to making money with your options trading.

Chapter 12: Day Trading and Swing Trading

Active traders place themselves in two groups – the day and swing traders. All are after one thing – to profit from short-term stock movements in the market. But which strategy is the best for you as a newbie? Let us look at these different t strategies so that you understand the differences.

Day Trading

As the name suggests, this is a form of trading that involves placing a number of trades in a day. The process is based on the use of charting systems and technical analysis. The objective of the day trader is to make money from trading various merchandise, stocks, currencies or my making little profit that will accumulate to become a major one. Day traders do not keep any position overnight – everything ends during the day.

The principal appeal of day trading is the would-be profits on many trades. However, this is only possible for that trader who has the different traits that include diligence, discipline, and decisiveness.

While many traders are advised against risking money that they can't afford to lose, a huge percentage of them end up incurring losses, especially on borrowed money. These losses end up curtailing their trading career and immerse them in debt.

Day traders work alone, independent of corporate influences. They have a flexible working schedule that allows them to take time off whenever they wish.

A day trader has to contend with hedge funds, high frequency trades and market professionals with the capacity to spend millions on trading platforms to gain an advantage. The trader spends heavily on purchasing a trading platform, computers, charting software and more.

Ongoing expenses include commission expenses, the cost of obtaining live price quotes and more.

To make it as a day trader, you need to watch multiple screens so that you can pinpoint trading opportunities then act fast to take advantage of them. The trader has to do this day after day, which makes the trader end up being burnt out.

Swing Trading

This mode of trading bases so much on identifying swings in commodities, stocks, and currencies that run over several days. The ideal swing trader takes a few days or weeks to complete the trade. Unlike a day trader, the swing trader has a low probability of making the trade a full-time career.

The longer time frame doesn't force the trader to stay glued to the computer screen all day long. The trader can sustain a full-time job and trade on the sides.

Trades need time to work out, and usually, it takes a few days or weeks for you to achieve higher profits compared to trading the same security several times a day.

Since swing trading involves positions that are held for more than 24 hours, the margin requirements are way higher.

Just like any other trading style, swing trading can lead to losses. Because swing traders cling to positions for way longer than day traders and they run the danger of bigger losses.

Since swing trading isn't a permanent job, there is a lower possibility of exhaustion due to stress. The best thing is that swing traders typically have a normal job or a source of income that can make up for trading losses.

You can run swing trading on just one computer and doesn't require state of the art technology for day trading.

The Key Differences Between Day Trading & Swing Trading

Day trading and swing trading both have rewards and drawbacks. Neither approach can be said to be superior to the other, and traders need to select a strategy that works best for their lifestyle, skills and other preferences. This form of trading is more suitable for persons who are keen about running trading on a permanent basis and have the prerequisites of day trading – discipline, extreme diligence, and decisiveness.

Day trading success also needs you to have an advanced understanding of charting and technical trading. Since the whole process is demanding and intense, traders are able to be calm knowing that they are working with facts. They can also control the emotions.

Finally, you need to understand that day trading has a lot of risks; you might end up losing all your investment if you aren't careful enough.

On the other hand, swing trading doesn't need such a wide mix of traits. Since it can be handled by anyone with enough funds and doesn't need you to be there all the time, the trader can keep their daytime jobs and run the trades on the side.

Swing trading accumulates losses and gains much more slowly compared to day trading, but there are also some instances when swing trades result in gains quickly.

Varying capital requirements also form a basis for both trading methods. Day trading in the US requires you to have at least an account balance of $25,000, while no legal minimum is required for Swing traders.

Both swing trading and day trading require a huge deal of work and knowledge of generating consistent profits. However, the knowledge required doesn't necessarily be "book smarts." A little knowledge on the market and a profitable strategy can start generating you some income, along with a lot of practice.

Chapter 13: Day Trading Training

Day training is a tough career. Whether you are an experienced trader or new to the field, you need to have a support network of other pro traders. Finding a training facility that offers mentoring and courses is an efficient way to get the knowledge to succeed in the markets. Many trading schools also offer online courses, group sessions, video conferencing and personal consultations.

The cost, support systems, and quality of the training varies from school to school; it is all about reviewing the various programs and come up with the best one to enroll.

Picking a Day Training school

To choose the best training facility to use for your training, you need to look at various aspects. The first element you need to consider is the cost of the training.

While the price is a huge factor to consider, you shouldn't make it the only factor. If you jump into a training school without any guidance, you find yourself losing a lot of money quickly. For instance, as a day trader you might end up losing all your trading funds ($25,000), which is a huge sum compared to paying just $3,000 to mitigate such losses.

Most institutions that offer training have three tenets that they focus on:

Foundation

This gives you the knowledge of the market that you wish to trade as well as the strategies that will help you to make profit from the market. While most of the strategies vary, you can opt to train via the web at little or no cost at all. Many trading institutions also give you a part of the training for free.

Mentoring

These come in the form of one-on-one coaching, webinars and trade critiques, and have turned out to be more effective compared to the information that you receive from articles or books.

The mentoring stage brings to the table an objective observer to help you trade better. The premise of mentoring is in such a way that it is easier for someone else to see the mistakes we do as traders compared to doing it alone. An expert takes time to look for and spot the errors and then correct you with the aim of providing a better way to trade.

Support

For many traders, slipping into bad habits happen very fast. Having a team or a school that helps you through this tricky time is a huge advantage. Remember that this is not just for newbies but established traders as well.

Top Day Trading Courses to Explore

Here, we look at a few online trading courses that are available for you to explore. We look at the content, the advantaged and disadvantages. At the end of it all, you get the chance to make the right choice.

Stock Trading Course

One of the most traded securities on the market is stocks. The price of stocks depends on the performance of the company as well as its expectations in future in term of performance.

Stock trading requires a lot of knowledge to make a profit. This is true especially for day trading where the securities are bought and sold intraday. The professional course allows you to have the information that reduces the time wastage and losses.

Good stock trading courses follow a definite learning path that is available for traders of different levels.

Learners are given an introduction into the work of the stock market and the trading mechanisms as well as what is needed.

Most of the trainers offer simulations of environments for you to perform trading demos.

Forex Trading Course

A Forex trader buys or sells one of the currency pairs via a brokerage platform, making profit from the changes in currency values. These changes are usually noticeable in decimal points.

Apart from changes in prices based on events, trading in currencies is characterized by varying trends. The trends can be calculated using expert tools. Forex trading classes are readily available online and form a god way to familiarize oneself with the subject.

You get to learn the basics of Forex trading, the trading platforms that you can use and what each offers.

Options Trading Courses

These are the so-called derivatives. This means that options are tied to the price of an underlying stock. The option puts you in a contract for you trade an asset such as a stock at an agreed price until a specified date.

Options are highly volatile products since the value is tied to a certain time frame and thus the price swings can be more marked than the stocks themselves.

Many institutions give you a simplified course for you to understand the complex world of options trading. You will learn about options trading terminology and the logistics, things to consider, understanding the option chain, spread on options and paper trading plan.

Futures Trading Course

Futures are slightly similar to options – they consist of an agreement between the seller and the buyer regarding a transaction at a predefined time and price. For options, the buyer is free to waive the right to sell and buy, while futures give the trader the option to sell and buy in a mutual agreement.

The risks for the buyer are a lot since he has to buy at the agreed time and price regardless of the results.

It is therefore ideal to understand the various mechanisms of futures trading before you enter into it. You can access this complex subject by attending online classes.

Benefits of Hands-on Day Trade Training

This encompasses practical experience and hands on training to help you grasp the basics and advanced trade skills. This method has a number of advantages when you graduate from being a student to a trader. Here are the top benefits to expect:

• Active on-job Problem Solving Skills

Day trading requires a lot of active problem solving, often without having a handbook to refer to. During this time, you get to engage deeply with concepts and materials, which prepares you much better for the real world.

• High levels of Materials Knowledge

Imagine trying to do some tasks from a book, tasks that need you to touch and engage with the trainer. When you learn through hands-on learning, you get to understand the way everything functions.

• Improved Memory

Studies on the efficacy of various training types found out that hands-on training offers a higher level of student retention than other training environments. Studies show that students only retain 20 percent of information if it is presented in lecture format, while many students retained 75 percent of the information they learn firsthand.

While each individual has the capacity to learn differently, interacting directly with the systems and concept lead to greater practical memories of the lessons. A large part of the improved retention result is due to the various practice opportunities you get when you use hands on training.

• Mentorship and Apprenticeship Opportunities

In any trading environment, most of the learning comes from the experience that others have gained. After training, they can offer mentorship and apprenticeship opportunities with other companies.

These opportunities allow you to work with an expert in the field and learn directly from their experience.

Mentorship opportunities usually lead to employment opportunities once you complete the course.

Chapter 14: Common Day Trading Myths

In the digital world we live in, it is never wise to listen to everything that you hear. Some information delivered over the internet is simply meant to blind you from reality. Other facts are there to mislead you. With regards to day trading, there are certain myths which have been there for years now. Some of these myths are just stories meant to deter people from earning profits through this lucrative trading activity. If you are new to trading, it is essential for you to know some of these myths and ways in which you could distinguish them from the truth. This section unveils common myths that you might have heard about day trading.

Day Trading is Similar to Gambling

A huge misconception that most people have in mind about day trading is thinking that this activity is similar to gambling. If you mention this to an experienced investor, the chances are that they might punch you in the face. This is because this myth is far from the truth. Day trading is not gambling. Gambling is purely based on luck. On the other hand, trading will depend on your rationality and reason. You have to set your emotions aside to ensure that you successfully trade. Also, you should realize that with day trading, there are no fast profits to expect. Contrarily, this is what most gamblers expect from their gambling activity. You need to get it clear that trading is not similar to gambling. Don't be swayed to believing that this is true.

It Is A Man's Game

You shouldn't be surprised if you come across such a myth. Trading is not something that only men can engage in. Many traders out there are women. Just because you think that there is a huge risk tied to day trading doesn't mean that it's a man's game. No! In fact, there are traders who often argue that the best investors in day trading are women. So, don't make assumptions based on hearsay.

You Will Lose Everything

Honestly, how can you lose everything when you are using the risk management tips which have been discussed in this manual? Most people who fail in day trading enter the market without any plan. Also, a good number of them allow their emotions to get the most out of them. As a result, they end up making decisions which affect their finances terribly. It could also be that they lack disciple to stick to their strategies. Having a strategy is not just enough to guarantee that you limit your losses and grow your profits. You need to walk the talk by implementing the plan.

Stops Are Not Necessary

Some might lead you into believing that the idea of using stops only shows that you are too afraid to take risks. Well, this is also far from the truth. The truth of the matter is that stops are tools which help to save you from losing all your capital in a single mistake that you make. Sometimes it is better to live to fight tomorrow. Hence, you need always to embrace the idea of using stops at all times.

Trading All Day Makes Your Earn More Money

From the different strategies which you will be implementing, you will realize that there are good and bad times to trade. Hence, it is basically unreasonable to think that one could make more money trading all day. Most traders prefer to trade in the morning since they could take advantage of high market volatility during these periods. Others prefer to trade at different times. So, trading all day does not guarantee you make more money. As a matter of fact, you could feasibly take on more losses since there is no guarantee in day trading.

Allowing Your Wins to Run

Day trading newbies will believe that the best way of making a fortune from their good trades is by allowing them to continue running. One thing that should be made clear is that you can only make money once you sell the securities you are trading. Therefore, allowing your wins to run is not safe. Anything can happen when market prices fall drastically. It could be worse when you had stepped outside for a break waiting to make a fortune from your investments. For that reason, you should always acknowledge the importance of taking profits where necessary. Don't be greedy.

Leverage is Bad

Some traders who have failed in the industry would argue that leverage is bad. Certainly, if you use leverage for all the wrong reasons, it will have a detrimental effect on your trading business. Essentially, leverage is a tool which helps you purchase more securities without funds. Therefore, if you employ a good strategy to trade, you could end up making a lot, thanks to leverage from your trader.

One Must Have A Huge Bankroll

Clearly, from what has been discussed, there are varying amounts of capital which you will require depending on the market you choose to trade. This means that the myth of having a huge bankroll for you to trade doesn't apply. With as little as $1,000, you can begin online trading. You should, however, be careful when limiting yourself to a certain amount. If you want to earn good returns, you have to be willing to risk.

You Don't Need Any Rules

Another misconception which you will come across is that you don't need to stick to any day trading rules. Picture a scenario where a soccer game is played without any rules. Undeniably, this would be utterly confusing. Day trading is just the same. Without rules, you will only incur losses. Ultimately, you will give up the perception that day trading doesn't work. Therefore, it is vital for you to have rules which help you to maintain your discipline.

Knowing that there are several myths which could deter you from knowing the truth about day trading is significant. With some in-depth research into this topic, you will garner a deeper understanding of the possible benefits which could accrue as you trade. Don't believe anything that you hear. Always make sure you do your homework before entering any trading market.

Conclusion

Thank for making it through to the end of this book, let's hope it was informative and able to provide you with all of the tools you need to achieve your goals whatever they may be.

The next step is to learn a few strategies and master them as well as you can. The strategies that you are most comfortable with should then be practiced on a demo account. Most brokers offer demo accounts so find a broker and begin practicing. You should practice as often as possible in order to perfect the strategy. Once you feel confident enough, you can then begin trading at the markets using your own funds. You should then start earning lots of money within a relatively short period of time.

Finally, if you found this book useful in any way, a review is always appreciated!

Don't miss out!

Visit the website below and you can sign up to receive emails whenever Michael Branson publishes a new book. There's no charge and no obligation.

https://books2read.com/r/B-A-MWSI-NPNAB

BOOKS 2 READ

Connecting independent readers to independent writers.

Did you love *Day Trading For Beginners Learn The Best Strategies On How To Profit Using Trading Tactics, Tools, Psychology, Money Management And Generate Passive Income*? Then you should read *Swing Trading A Beginners And Advanced Guide For Effective Trading Tactics, Make More Money And Reach Financial Freedom* by Michael Branson!

Swing trading can be a fun and very lucrative way to make a living off the stock market. While it's slower paced than day trading, it does require that you have some tolerance for risk, that you're willing to do technical analysis of the stock market and understand what you're doing, and that you use sound judgment and don't "risk it all" for the sake of a single trade.

If you follow the principles outlined in this book, you are on your way to becoming a successful swing trader and I hope that you have found the presentation in this book to be helpful, practical, and useful.

Think of swing trading as a business, and that will help ensure your success. Owning a business means you take reasonable risks and guard your capital. We have discussed ways to do that in the book, and I hope that you don't give in to all the common mistakes made by beginners. It can be too easy to give into emotion when trading on the stock market and large amounts of money are on the line. Don't fall prey to that temptation.

I wish the best of luck to everyone who read this book.

What are you waiting for? Download your copy today!

Also by Michael Branson

Swing Trading A Beginners And Advanced Guide For Effective Trading Tactics, Make More Money And Reach Financial Freedom Day Trading For Beginners Learn The Best Strategies On How To Profit Using Trading Tactics, Tools, Psychology, Money Management And Generate Passive Income

CPSIA information can be obtained
at www.ICGtesting.com
Printed in the USA
BVHW031403220819
556561BV00001B/60/P